NEHEMIAH

THE HOLY CITY

10 Publishing
a division of 10 of those.com

First published in Great Britain in 2017

British Library Cataloguing in Publication Data

A record for this book is available from the British Library

ISBN: 978-1-911272-67-0
Designed by Diane Warnes
Printed in the UK

10Publishing, a division of 10ofthose.com
Unit C, Tomlinson Road, Leyland, PR25 2DY, England
Email: info@10ofthose.com
Website: www.10ofthose.com

Chris Young

31 UNDATED DEVOTIONS THROUGH THE BOOK OF NEHEMIAH

INTRODUCTION

The meaning of Nehemiah's name – 'The LORD has comforted' – is very appropriate. This is a book about 'the great and awesome' God (1:5; 4:14; 9:32) who comforts his people with his faithfulness. The God who is unchanging, unshakable and gracious far beyond anything that we deserve. The God of the Bible.

Here are three big questions to ask as we read Nehemiah:

1. Where are we in salvation history? That's always vital when we read any part of the Bible: where have we reached in the unfolding of God's plans and purposes? How are the promises of God to the people of God – the promises to and through Abraham, Moses, David and the prophets – progressing? What has been fulfilled? What is still lacking?

2. How does the book model faith to us (that is, living rightly as God's people by taking God at his word)? Nehemiah himself is a truly remarkable man of God, as we will see! We have much to learn from him. We also find the Jews acting together in faith as a people, and there is plenty to apply to ourselves corporately as the church of Christ.

3. Most importantly, how does the book point us to the Lord Jesus? As Nehemiah seeks to build a 'new Jerusalem', he foreshadows the words and work of a far greater man of God. The purpose of all God-breathed Scripture is to make us wise for salvation through faith in Christ Jesus, and to equip us for godly lives in his service (2 Tim. 3:15–17). We've got the book wrong if we don't learn from it to love, trust, follow and obey Christ! And ultimately it should leave us crying, 'Come, Lord Jesus' (Rev. 22:20).

As we read Nehemiah, let's pray with Paul: 'Now may our Lord Jesus Christ himself, and God our Father, who loved us and gave us eternal comfort and good hope through grace, comfort your hearts and establish them in every good work and word.' (2 Thes. 2:16–17, ESV)

For those who are interested, more material on the background of the book of Nehemiah can be found at the end of these notes.

DAY 1

READ Nehemiah 1:1, 11b

Nehemiah Part 1: Restoring the Place

Much of what we call the book of Nehemiah is the writings of the man himself. First-person historical narrative is quite rare in the Old Testament, so the book has a very intense, personal feel. All that we know for sure about Nehemiah we learn from this book; he is not mentioned anywhere else in the Bible. But we will get to know this 'formidable, practical man'[1] quite well!

We start in a city called Susa, in what is now Iran. Susa was the winter capital of the Persian Empire. The date is autumn 446 BC, during the twentieth year of Emperor Artaxerxes I (we are reminded of the king's name in 2:1). This is the last history book of the Old Testament (Malachi, the latest Old Testament book of all, is set perhaps a decade after the end of Nehemiah).

What has become of God's people, Israel – the Jews, as they are now called? When Emperor Cyrus announced that the Jews could leave exile in Babylon and return to their homeland (Ezra 1) a good number went up to the land of Judah, first under the leadership of Zerubbabel and Joshua (Ezra 2). Later, another smattering came with Ezra (Ezra 8). But not all the Jews returned to the promised land. Many stayed in the places of exile (we read the story of some of them in the book of Esther, also set in Susa). Clearly Nehemiah's family is one of those that has remained.

And they have flourished in exile! Nehemiah is a significant person at court: cupbearer to the Persian emperor (v. 11b). Cupbearers were more than simply wine-tasters. They could often be trusted advisors, even friends, of the king. Nehemiah has done very well for himself.

The stage is set!

REFLECTION

None of what happens in Nehemiah happens by accident. We will see much more of this, but why not start by praising God that he ordains the movements of all nations, the destiny of his people, and the life of each individual (including yours!). Thank him that we have 'Nehemiah' in our Bibles!

DAY 2

READ Nehemiah 1:2–3

Hanani is probably a blood relation of Nehemiah (he appears again in 7:2). He arrives in Susa with a deputation from Judah. And Nehemiah is very keen to find out how things are going for the remnant who had returned to Jerusalem (v. 2).

That is remarkable in itself! Here is our first glimpse into the heart of Nehemiah the man. Jerusalem is 800 miles from Susa. Several generations have passed since the first Jews returned from exile. Nehemiah and his family have done well where they are. Jerusalem and the people there could so easily be out of sight, out of mind for Nehemiah. Why would he be bothered about them?

But Nehemiah is a man who loves the Lord and his people, and who knows his Scriptures. Of course he is bothered! He will go to great lengths for the good of these people.

There is a challenge for us there. But perhaps we also get just a little pre-echo of another one who held the highest possible position of privilege – and yet was concerned for a people very far off in every sense! Paul tells us about him in Philippians 2:5–11.

The news from Jerusalem is all bad, though. Long gone are the glorious days of David and Solomon. Even the hopes of a great renewal after the exile, as promised by the prophets, seem dashed. The people of God are a pitiful few, living in a tribute territory to a pagan king, their city in ruins. And there are plenty of other problems, as we will see. 'Great trouble and disgrace' (v. 3) is the painful reality.

REFLECTION

'... remember those in prison as if you were together with them in prison, and those who are ill-treated as if you yourselves were suffering' (Heb. 13:3). How bothered are we about God's church across the world? Whether it is desperately compromised? Or desperately persecuted? How does Nehemiah challenge us – and point us to Jesus?

DAY 3

READ Nehemiah 1:4–7

Nehemiah is absolutely devastated by the news from Jerusalem. He weeps over Jerusalem – as Jesus, equally devastated by the disgrace of God's people, will himself do a few centuries later (Luke 19:41–44).

Godly man that he is, Nehemiah's first response is to pray. We will find him praying all through the book. We can learn so much by studying the prayers recorded in the Bible, and what a wonderful prayer we have here!

Nehemiah begins by lifting his eyes to the God of heaven: the great, awesome, faithful, covenant God (v. 5). We should not be too quick to begin with ourselves when we pray! This is a God-centred prayer in a God-centred book. Trouble does not lead Nehemiah to doubt God's sovereign faithfulness. Quite the opposite: it leads him to remind himself of the truth.

But dwelling on the glory of God always reminds us of how far short we fall of his glory. Nehemiah knows why all this trouble and shame has come upon God's people. The root cause is sin – their disobedience to God's word (v. 7). So he earnestly confesses to God the sin of Israel, including his family's and his own (v. 6).

What a deep sense of the horror of sin Nehemiah has. Sin in 'the world' is evil enough. But sin like this amongst those who call themselves God's people is far worse.

When was the last time we prayed like this? Previous generations of Christians have perhaps been better at owning and acknowledging sin. Has the ease and selfishness of the culture we live in dulled us? We get upset about all sorts of things. But do we really echo the words of the Book of Common Prayer: 'We acknowledge and bewail our manifold sins and wickedness ... The remembrance of them is grievous unto us; the burden of them is intolerable. Have mercy upon us, have mercy upon us, most merciful Father ...'? Let us not lose a right sense of the vileness of sin before a holy God.

REFLECTION

Let Nehemiah's confession challenge us to genuine confession of sin.

DAY 4

READ Nehemiah 1:8–11a

The only hope for God's people in this mess is for God himself to do something. Having confessed, Nehemiah now makes his request to God (something which only forgiven people may do!): 'Remember' (v. 8). 'Remember' is a covenant word. When God 'remembers' in the Bible, it is not that he is recalling something he has forgotten (as if!), but rather that he is *acting* on what he has already promised.[2]

And so, in verses 8–10, Nehemiah prays God's own words back to him – you can't go far wrong in prayer if you do that! It's a covenant prayer. He echoes passages like Deuteronomy 30:1–10, and many others. These were the promises that God made through Moses to the people he had just brought out of Egypt (see v. 10; cf. Deut. 9:29). As Derek Kidner writes, 'At this point Israel had been threatened with extinction; now, it seems, Nehemiah sees the situation as hardly less perilous. Like Moses, he must stand in the breach with his intercession.'[3] This, of course, is supremely what Jesus will do!

Nehemiah knows that God hears the prayers of his 'servants who delight in revering your name' (v. 11 – how often do we think of ourselves like that?!) So he is humble, but confident, as he asks for success in the sight of the king. He is planning to make a bold request.

In effect, Nehemiah is praying, 'Lord, please do what you have said you will do!' He is a man who knows his Bible, and allows God's word to shape his prayers. Although some things have changed for new-covenant believers – the shadows have given way to the realities – we would struggle to find a better model of praying than to pray earnestly with Nehemiah: 'Your will be done!' Our Lord Jesus prayed that too (Luke 22:42).

REFLECTION

How much of our praying is shaped by the priorities of God's word – the things that he has said he wants to happen? Do we pray most for the gospel going out to the lost, for the maturity of believers and ultimately for the return of Jesus?

DAY 5

READ Nehemiah 2:1–8

Nisan is the first month of the next Jewish year. This means that Nehemiah has been praying for four months (the events of chapter 1 took place in Kislev, the ninth month of the previous year, 1:1)! But now it's time to act.

Nehemiah has wisely waited very carefully for the right occasion. Artaxerxes I ruled the Persian Empire from 465–424 BC. He called himself 'king of kings'![4] Artaxerxes is sharp-minded and clearly used to asking direct questions (see vv. 2, 4, 6)! He is a man to be taken seriously. No wonder Nehemiah is 'very much afraid' (v. 2).

He has another reason to tremble. Just a few years earlier, this same Artaxerxes had ordered an attempt to rebuild the wall of Jerusalem to stop (see Ezra 4:7–23). He must ask the king to reverse his own decree!

On the other hand, Nehemiah knows that twelve years before, Artaxerxes had allowed Ezra to go to Jerusalem, and had granted him all the resources he needed at royal expense (see Ezra 7). Most importantly, Nehemiah also knows who is truly on the throne!

So – after a hasty prayer (v. 4)! – he carefully makes his request, getting more confident as the king appears favourable (vv. 5–8). But note how respectful he is (vv. 3, 5, 7). There is never any place for believers to dishonour ruling authorities, as the New Testament makes very clear (cf. Paul's words in Acts 26:24–29). Nehemiah is courteous – but bold: bold to seek the good of God's people from an unbelieving king.

His courage and faith are rewarded; every request is granted. But notice to whom Nehemiah attributes the success, God (v. 8), who is sovereign even over the heart of the so-called 'king of kings' (Prov. 21:1.).

REFLECTION

Knowing that God is sovereign, how might we today, prayerfully and humbly, seek the good of God's people from the authorities placed over us?

DAY 6

READ Nehemiah 2:9–20

With the king's protection, Nehemiah makes the long journey to Jerusalem (vv. 9, 11). In secret, he goes out at night to inspect the walls (vv. 12–16). He does not tell anyone yet what he is planning – again we see a wise and shrewd thinker, surveying how the land lies (literally) without making any rash moves.

But he is not afraid to tell it like it is! He now confronts the people of Jerusalem with their sin and failure, and urges them to address it (v. 17). Yet neither does he forget to encourage them with God's grace and sovereignty (v. 18). The realisation of both sin and grace is always vital for true repentance! Nehemiah continues to identify with them, saying 'we' and 'us'. He knows he too must continue to live God's ways.

He receives a mixed reception. Some – under God's sovereign hand – 'strengthened their hands for the good work' (v. 18, ESV). But we also see the first sign of opposition as both Sanballat and Tobiah are enraged 'that someone had come to promote the welfare of the Israelites' (v. 10). That is very chilling! They, and 'Geshem the Arab', also mock and falsely accuse Nehemiah and the people of sedition (v. 19). (The reader knows in fact that Nehemiah has the king's personal approval.) This is not the last we will see of these men. But notice Nehemiah's robust response: those who are truly God's will serve him and be blessed; but his enemies' final end is to have no part in the people of God (v. 20). Woe to them!

Jesus himself received the same reception, when he came from heaven itself to offer us fullness of grace through the cross – if only we turn to him from our sin. Some joyfully responded in repentance and faith. Others raged (Luke 6:11), falsely accused (Luke 23:2), and mocked (Luke 23:35–37). Anyone who follows Christ must expect the same reaction.

REFLECTION

Jesus says, 'Whoever wants to be my disciple must deny themselves and take up their cross daily and follow me' (Luke 9:23). Pray that by grace you would daily walk in repentance and faith.

DAY 7

READ Nehemiah 3:1–32

Chapter 3 is a list of those who knuckled down and rebuilt the wall. Some of what happens in chapters 4–6 occurs during the building, which took about seven weeks, as we learn in 6:15.

The list runs anticlockwise around Jerusalem, from the Sheep Gate in verse 1 back round to the Sheep Gate in verse 32! It names each person or group who builds; generally, each of them rebuilds the part of the wall nearest to where they live or work.

Why is this list – the first of several in the book – here? The most striking thing is the sheer diversity of the people named. It is not just workmen who build. There are priests – including the high priest (v. 1), Levites (v. 17), goldsmiths and perfumers (v. 8), the rich and powerful (vv. 9, 17), even foreigners (v. 7), and a family effort in verse 12 – daughters included! Rich, poor, old, young, 'gifted' at this particular service or not ... they could easily fall out about so much. But they work side by side in the service of God – and in response to a godly leader. What an answer to Nehemiah's prayer!

Almost the whole tiny population of Jerusalem mucked in; it needed all of them. Here is a glimpse of what the corporate people of God should be like when we get our thinking right. Remember Paul's words: 'Here there is no Gentile or Jew, circumcised or uncircumcised, barbarian, Scythian, slave or free, but Christ is all, and is in all' (Col. 3:11).

The one sour note comes in verse 5. There are always some who will not stoop to serve. Let that not be us!

REFLECTION

'Building' is a big New Testament theme! Jesus, the great man of God, also came to build (Matt. 16:18); those who are truly God's people respond and build too – on Christ himself, the cornerstone. Ponder Paul's words about building in Ephesians 2:19–22 and 4:15–16.

DAY 8

READ Nehemiah 4:1–6

Sanballat and Tobiah are still furious at what's going on. Sanballat appears to have military support (v. 2) – Nehemiah's enemies are powerful men! Nehemiah is a threat to their position, and they do not like this upstart from Susa one bit. (King Herod would react similarly to Jesus' birth centuries later – see Matthew 2.) Once again, Sanballat and Tobiah attempt to derail the building project by mockery and pathetic insult (vv. 1–3).

Nehemiah responds with prayer (vv. 4–5), and perseverance (v. 6). His prayer (and others like it in the Old Testament) might sound unsettling to us. But we should remember that this is again a covenant prayer. God had always promised that he would destroy Israel's enemies. Nehemiah prays for God to do as he has said he will do. He also knows that, ultimately, the offended party is God, 'Do not cover their guilt, and let not their sin be blotted out from your sight, for they have provoked you to anger in the presence of the builders (v.5, ESV). Opposition to God's people is always an expression of hatred towards God himself. The enemies of Israel are the enemies of God. Nehemiah, as we know, is very concerned for the honour of the Lord. So – perhaps remembering Deuteronomy 32:34–43 – he rightly leaves judgement to God, knowing that God is more than capable of upholding the honour of his name!

Things are not so different for new-covenant believers. God still promises to destroy our enemies – something of which Paul reminds the beleaguered Thessalonians for their encouragement (2 Thes. 1:5–12). When God's kingdom comes, it always comes with both salvation and judgement; and unrepentant opposition to God and his people can only end in judgement.

We should remember that whenever we pray 'your kingdom come'! When Christ returns, his enemies will be judged – to his glory.

Threats are ineffective in the face of united trust in the Lord, so the Israelites build on (v. 6). And so should we!

REFLECTION

As we wait for Jesus to come back, we live in a 'tension' between longing for the lost – even the most ferocious opponents of the gospel (Acts 7:60) – to be saved, and longing for Christ to finally destroy his enemies. How might our praying rightly reflect this tension?

DAY 9

READ Nehemiah 4:7–14

Tobiah and Sanballat are not going to give up – and the list of powerful enemies is growing (v. 7). Jerusalem is surrounded literally on every side.[5] Now the opposition turns much more serious (v. 8). Words having proved ineffective, they resort to planning violence. When we, God's people, persevere, our opponents rarely give up and go home! In fact, the more we persevere, the more opposition tends to intensify.

The wall is only half-finished and the work is hard (v. 10). That, and word of the planned attack, seems to get to the Jews on the building project, causing a mid-point wobble in morale (vv. 11–12). You sense the tension and uncertainty here. The work is under serious threat.

But Nehemiah is made of stern stuff. He reminds the Jews who is sovereign (v. 14). Yet there is no 'let go and let God' here. Verse 9 is well known for good reasons: 'But we prayed to our God and posted a guard day and night to meet this threat.' What a wonderful blend of dependence and determination. He is not a man of action without prayer. Nor is he a man of prayer without action. (Jesus himself would talk about being both prayerful and watchful – see, for example, Mark 14:38).

Nehemiah makes a bold and decisive move, ensuring that the builders are secure, armed and ready to fight (v. 13). Then he tells them to get on with the battle (v. 14)! Surrounded by a hostile world, they put their trust in God, and persevere (cf. John 16:33).

What a model Nehemiah is for us in so many ways! All Christians could learn much from his prayerfulness, his knowledge of the Scriptures, and his zeal for God's name. But his own rich spiritual life doesn't lead to smug laziness. It leads to whole-hearted, courageous, unashamed service to God and his people.

REFLECTION

God's sovereignty never cancels out our responsibility, nor vice versa. Nehemiah understood that! Do we?

DAY 10

READ Nehemiah 4:15–23

The threat has been staved off, for now at least. Notice to whom Nehemiah gives the credit: 'God had frustrated' their plot (v. 15). But Nehemiah is no fool; this is no time to become complacent. He establishes a permanent arrangement of armed builders, each person carrying weapons in a way that means they can still work (vv. 16–20). Again we see Nehemiah's plain common sense and clear thinking. We also see his godliness: he reminds them once more that God will uphold them (v. 20). Perhaps he is thinking of Psalm 127:1: 'Unless the LORD watches over the city, the guards stand watch in vain.'

What a tireless encourager Nehemiah is! We would do well to learn from his example of encouraging others to 'remember the Lord' (v. 14), and that 'our God will fight for us!' (v. 20). The true people of God respond eagerly to such godly leadership (vv. 21–23) – they always do! Much heartened, they labour night and day on the wall. Nehemiah himself is of course right at the forefront.

The New Testament makes it clear that God's people are no longer a geographical nation. So usually there is no need for physical walls or armour! But our enemies are still very real, and so is our spiritual battle. Hence Paul tell us too to be fully armed and ready to fight in the strength that Christ supplies (Eph. 6:10–20). Church leaders must remind God's people of these things – and demonstrate them in their lives!

REFLECTION

Nehemiah urges the slightly flagging people of God to keep at it! Paul also urges us: 'Let us not become weary in doing good, for at the proper time we will reap a harvest if we do not give up' (Gal. 6:9).

DAY 11

READ Nehemiah 5:1–13

Nehemiah takes a break from the story of the wall – perhaps to build suspense! And he shows us in chapter 5 that the enemies outside are not the only threat to this little people of God. There is danger within too: sin and compromise.

Times are hard (vv. 2–3). Nehemiah discovers that the richer Jews – especially the officials and nobles – are extorting money from the poorer ones and exacting interest (v. 7). They are even enslaving them (v. 5), or selling them to the nations to be sold back to the rich Jews again (v. 8)! All of this is totally against God's commands on how they were to treat one another (see Lev. 25:35–46). This simply should not be the case amongst God's people. In the face of famine, the Jews should have been sharing with one another. (Just in case we think this is an 'Old Testament thing,' note 1 John 3:17!)

The pre-exile prophets pointed forward to a great time of renewal and faithfulness after the exile. This doesn't seem to square with the reality, as the post-exile prophets (Haggai, Zechariah, and Malachi) confirm. The people of Judah are just as sinful as they ever were.

We have already seen in chapter 1 how seriously Nehemiah views sin amongst God's people. He is furious (v. 6). He wisely collects himself and then acts, bravely challenging the leaders of the Jews (v. 7). He points out the horrid irony (v. 8), reminds them how this exploitation dishonours God (v. 9), and calls on them all to repent (vv. 10–11) – once again sharing the blame and taking the lead in repentance.

The response in verses 12–13 is remarkable! Genuine, joyful, committed repentance seems to take place. That, as ever, is the right response.

Nehemiah deals with their sin – to an extent. But it will take someone far greater to sort out sin completely.

REFLECTION

The twin dangers of 'external opposition' and 'internal compromise' are an ever-present threat to the church – read the events of Acts 4–5, or the letters to the churches in Revelation 2–3. We should be aware that attacks will come from both – and we should be ready.

DAY 12

READ Nehemiah 5:14–19

As many people have pointed out, Nehemiah is very far from being simply 'the book on how to do Christian leadership'! But that isn't to say we can't learn about Christian leadership from him; there is much he teaches us.

Nehemiah is no fraud. He has just challenged the officials and nobles not to abuse their position. But he does not just 'talk the talk'. He models godly authority completely. During his twelve years as governor, he makes no use of his allowance (v. 14), acquires no land (v. 16), and feeds a large number of people each day at his own expense (vv. 17–18). Times are tough; lesser men would – and did – exploit others to feather their own nests. But, selfless man that he is, Nehemiah will not 'lord it over the people' (v. 15). Instead, he fears God (v. 15), and longs only for God's approval (v. 19).

Anyone in Christian leadership would benefit from pondering and following his example – and comparing it to the life of Paul in 1 Corinthians 9 (isn't Nehemiah so like Paul?!), or the words of Peter (1 Pet. 5:1–5). Indeed, any Christian would benefit from following Nehemiah's example (Heb. 13:7).

But Nehemiah's example does not point us ultimately to Nehemiah himself – nor does Paul's or Peter's! They are examples for us as they point us to follow in Christ's footsteps.

These verses also give us a great shadow of Jesus' sacrifice for us. Even though he was 'in very nature God,' he 'did not consider equality with God something to be used to his own advantage' (Phil. 2:6). Out of love for his Father and 'for the joy that was set before him he endured the cross' (Heb. 12:2). His supreme act of selfless service means that we who trust in him will even be served by him at his table (Luke 12:37)! Before we can even think about serving him, we must be served – and saved – by him.

REFLECTION

Ponder the parallels between these verses and Mark 10:35–45 – and be thankful!

DAY 13

READ Nehemiah 6:1–9

The wall is almost finished (v. 1). Perhaps Nehemiah's enemies will finally throw in the towel? Not a bit of it. In fact, chapter 6 is perhaps the 'high point' of opposition!

Finding that armed violence is clearly not working, Sanballat, Tobiah and Geshem decide to go straight for Nehemiah himself, in an attempt to 'cut the head off the snake'. They send him a message, winsomely inviting him to come and meet them ... a long way from Jerusalem, in an isolated spot (v. 2)! Nehemiah is far too savvy for that. He can smell a rat immediately, and rebuffs their repeated efforts (vv. 3–4).

So they try a different tack. They send an open letter to the Jews in Jerusalem, trying to sow doubts in their minds about Nehemiah's motives (vv. 6–7). They report accusations of rebellion, and even of a bid by Nehemiah to make himself king! Of course the readers know that none of it is true – as Nehemiah curtly points out (v. 8).

Many Christian leaders face these same kind of lies directed against them. The apostle Paul did. And so too did Jesus! How does Nehemiah deal with such wicked deceit? He continues to pray (v. 9). His impressive success with the wall could easily lead to pride. But he will not let his spiritual guard down. He knows he needs to rely, each day, on God's gracious strength. We find even our Lord Jesus praying at moments of trouble or temptation. How much more do we need to be prayerful!

REFLECTION

Nehemiah knows he hasn't overcome his enemies by his own greatness, but by prayerful trust in the grace and power of God. Paul also urges us not to let our spiritual guard down: 'Continue steadfastly in prayer, being watchful in it with thanksgiving' (Col. 4:2, ESV).

DAY 14

READ Nehemiah 6:10–14

God's enemies are nothing if not persistent. Remember how the Pharisees kept throwing trick question after trick question at Jesus to see if they could finally trip him up!

Tobiah and Sanballat try an altogether more subtle, and more dangerous, approach. They hire a man to give what seems like a friendly warning (v. 10, cf. Luke 20:20!). But Nehemiah is having none of it; he can tell it's false (vv. 12–13a). How?

First, it's suspicious. Shemaiah, who is allegedly very housebound, is suggesting a meeting in the temple (v. 10)!

Second, Nehemiah has a God-given task (v. 11a). He's not going to run away from it, whether the threat is real or not! (Think too of Jesus resolutely setting his face to go to Jerusalem, to the cross, cf. Luke 9:51.)

Third, and most importantly, Nehemiah refuses because he knows his Scriptures. Shemaiah suggests meeting in the temple sanctuary – behind the temple doors. But according to the Law, only priests were allowed to go in there (Num. 18:7). Nehemiah is not a priest and can see at once that to enter the temple would be to sin (vv. 11b, 13b).

Shemaiah's invitation must be false and Nehemiah rejects it – riskily, but rightly. What courageous faith!

There have always been many false teachers and false brothers to threaten the church. (Nehemiah mentions more in verse 14!) Very often their teaching will be dressed up in winsome, spiritual language, like Shemaiah's in verse 10. This is Satan's most dangerous form of attack. How will we discern truth from lies? How else but by knowing our Bibles!

REFLECTION

Sugar-coated lies are the oldest trick of the devil and his servants (2 Cor. 11:13–15). He attempted to deceive Adam and Eve like this – and they fell for it. He tried the same trick with Jesus. But Jesus, standing firm on God's word, sent him packing (Luke 4:1–13). Praise Jesus!

DAY 15

READ Nehemiah 6:15 – 7:3

The wall is finished (6:15, 7:1). What a miraculous achievement! The people have worked hard, as God has enabled them. (That is the normal pattern of Christian life – Phil. 2:12–13.) Every attempt to stop the building has failed. Enemies have been slowly gathering in greater numbers all around, but this only means that more and more people can see what God has done!

But Tobiah, full of hate, has not given up hope of bringing down Nehemiah himself. It's now revealed that Tobiah has a foothold in the people of Judah because of his significant family ties (6:18) – as does Sanballat, we learn in 13:28. Tobiah is still dangerous, and still at his old tricks (6:19).

Knowing this, and knowing that their enemies might not remain in awe for long, Nehemiah takes some wise and godly practical steps. He appoints God-fearing leaders (7:2; cf. Tit. 1:5–9), and orders that the new gates be guarded and locked at night (7:3). He safeguards God's people against the attacks of their enemies.

There are plenty of lessons there! But as we finish this 'half' of the book, dealing with this man of God, his task, and his opponents, we should again consider Jesus.

Satan threw absolutely everything he had at Jesus: opposition from Jewish and Roman authorities; evil spirits out in force; temptations to sin, or to quit or to get sidetracked; and opposition from inside: deserting disciples, the Satan-filled Judas, and even Peter! The devil threw the kitchen sink at Jesus, but the Lord Jesus crushed him. He had no hold on Christ.

And by dying on the cross in our place, Jesus ensured that the people of God – those who have faith in Christ – will be eternally secure, because 'there is now no condemnation for those who are in Christ Jesus' (Rom. 8:1).

REFLECTION

It would be a big mistake to end this part of Nehemiah without a fresh trust in, a fresh commitment to following, and a fresh wonder, love and praise for Jesus Christ.

Nehemiah Part 2: Restoring the People

These verses are a transitional section. Up till now, the focus has mostly been on the physical rebuilding of Jerusalem. Now the attention switches to the Jews themselves. We move from the rebuilding of the *place* of God to the rebuilding of the *people* of God. (The two are inseparable, of course!)

The city is 'large and spacious' (v. 4), but it is almost empty of people. So Nehemiah does not now put his feet up and enjoy a well-earned rest. We are never done with serving God! The next task is to refill Jerusalem with people living under God's word. He starts by rooting round in the archives to see what has already been achieved – reminding us, as ever, that it is really God's work (v. 5).

Verses 6–73 are an almost exact re-run of Ezra 2. They list the very first people who came up out of exile, under the leadership of Zerubbabel and Joshua (v. 7). (Note that the Nehemiah in v. 7 is a different one to 'our' Nehemiah.) As this was now almost 100 years ago, the people of Jerusalem in Nehemiah's day are the grandchildren and great-grandchildren of these people.

Why does Nehemiah dig out this bit of history? Well, first it reminds us of those who responded in faith to God's call to return to the promised land (see Ezra 1:5). We are encouraged by the example of former saints.

But second, it reminds us that little has been done in the years since. The number that returned was pitifully small – 42,360 (v. 66), compared to the over half a million men that came out of 'exile' in Egypt (Num. 1:46)! – and it is still small in Nehemiah's day. There is much work to be done.

REFLECTION

God promised Abraham that his descendants would be countless. So whenever we read a list that numbers the people of God, we know we are not there yet. We too are still waiting for that time. But be sure it will come (Rev. 7:9)!

DAY 17

READ Nehemiah 8:1–8

A different, unnamed narrator now takes up the story. The following chapters are full of great encouragements, as what appears to be a genuine revival takes place! Some of the 'Psalms of Ascents' (Ps. 120–134, especially 126) may well have been written at this time.

It all starts with God's word, as true revival must: 'the Book of the Law of Moses, which the LORD had commanded for Israel' is brought out (v. 1). Just days after the completion of the wall, the entire people (vv. 1–2) are united by a (surely God-given) longing to hear the Scriptures. In fact, they demand to be taught (v. 1). So Ezra (the same man after whom the book 'Ezra' is named) and his team joyfully stand on a platform (v. 4), and Ezra reads the Law to the assembly, who listen attentively … all morning (v. 3)!

Ezra and the Levites do more than simply read; they explain the meaning so that everyone can understand (vv. 7–8). (The two main roles of the priests were to maintain the sacrificial system and to teach God's word, Deut. 33:10, cf. 1 Tim. 4:13).[6] And the people respond rightly with reverent praise: 'all the people lifted their hands and responded, "Amen! Amen!" Then they bowed down and worshipped the LORD with their faces to the ground' (v. 6).

This public reading, teaching and responding to the Scriptures is, and always has been, a vital mark of a true church of God.

REFLECTION

It is not for nothing that Paul urges us, 'Let the word of Christ dwell in you richly' (Col. 3:16, ESV). The word of Christ – about Christ! – is the means by which we may keep going in him. Pray that this would be the case, not only for you individually, but corporately in your local church and amongst God's people across the world.

DAY 18

READ Nehemiah 8:9–12

We read that 'the people had been weeping as they listened to the words of the Law' (v. 9). Sometimes that is a very appropriate response to God's word. King Josiah responds similarly in 2 Kings 22, as do both Ezra and Nehemiah themselves on other occasions.

But Ezra and Nehemiah instruct the people that this is not the time for mourning because this is a holy day. It is the first day of the seventh month (8:2). The seventh month was the 'high point' of the Israelite year; before celebrating the Day of Atonement on the tenth day, they marked the first day of the seventh month with the Feast of Trumpets. Therefore, quoting Leviticus 23:23–25, Nehemiah correctly tells the people that it is a holy day of rest, of gathering, and of offering.

This is a time for rejoicing in the Lord: 'the joy of the LORD is your strength' (v. 10). It is not 'holy' to mourn when we are supposed to be rejoicing in the Lord! So Nehemiah tells them to go and celebrate, typically encouraging those who have more to share with those who don't. (Remember his own example in chapter 5.) The Levites back up Nehemiah's instruction (v. 11).

So the people go and rejoice, 'because they now understood the words that had been made known to them' (v. 12). It is always an occasion for joy in the Lord when God's people understand his word better. Apart from the return of Jesus, the church can desire nothing greater than to know God in his word!

REFLECTION

We do not read the Scriptures simply to know the Scriptures. That just leads to pride (think of the Pharisees!). We read the Scriptures to know the God who has spoken in them. Most of all, to know how we may be saved through faith in Jesus Christ and how we may live lives to please him (2 Tim. 3:14–17). Understanding that is a cause for joy indeed!

DAY 19

READ Nehemiah 8:13–18

The people continue to study the Scriptures on the second day (v. 13). They read instructions for the Feast of Booths (or Tabernacles). This was one of the three main feasts in the Jewish year, when all the men were to go up to Jerusalem[7] – which makes it all the more shocking that it hasn't been done properly since the time of Joshua (v. 17)!

The feast was to be marked by two things. First, it was for remembrance. Israel was commanded to live in temporary shelters for a week, reminding them of their wanderings in the desert (Lev. 23:33–43). They were to remember God's wonderful salvation – but also his judgement on those who did not believe. 'Note then the kindness and the severity of God', as Paul puts it (Rom. 11:22, ESV).

Second, the feast was to be observed with rejoicing in the God of their redemption. The people gladly keep the feast: 'And their joy was very great' (v. 17)!

Sometimes when we read the Old Testament we need to distinguish between *practice* and *principle*. That is true here. The new-covenant people of God are also commanded to remember and to rejoice – the principle is the same. Yet this is not because of our rescue from slavery in Egypt but because of the real rescue from sin and all its consequences by the cross of Christ. So our 'practice' is different: we do not need to dwell under canvas for a week each year! But we do have our own 'visual aids' – Jesus left us with a supper which we 'do ... in remembrance of me' (1 Cor. 11:25), and in which we rejoice in the gospel. We should treasure this.

Nehemiah 8 is not the original institution of the feast, but a recommitment to it. So do we too need reminders to remember what God has done for us and to rejoice in it? Most definitely. And often!

REFLECTION

We are so prone to forget what God has done for us in Christ! How might we encourage one another to keep remembering and rejoicing?

DAY 20

READ Nehemiah 9:1–6

We've seen how Nehemiah is a real man of prayer. Perhaps some of his prayerfulness has rubbed off on the people under his leadership (that is not uncommon!) for in chapter 9 the people of Israel intercede together. Their prayer takes a very similar form to Nehemiah's own in chapter 1.

A few weeks have passed (v. 1). The people come together in clothes of mourning to confess their sins. Earlier in the month, they had been told not to mourn or weep – it was time for rejoicing. But confession has its right place too.

Once again they read from the Scriptures (v. 3). The best way to pray is always with our Bibles open. How God's word exposes us for what we are! They respond rightly: 'in confession and in worshipping the LORD their God'.

What is striking is how much time the people spend on this: half a day, according to verse 3! They are taking this very seriously. Perhaps we should be challenged by these ancestors in the faith, their priorities, their humility, and their eagerness to listen to the Lord and respond to him.

Nehemiah began his prayer by fixing his eyes on 'the great and awesome God' (Neh. 1:5). As the Levites lead the people in prayer, they do exactly the same; they praise God's glory and sovereignty over creation (9:5–6). That is a great encouragement to them in their weakness. And no less for us!

Where else would true believing prayer start but with God? As Jesus himself said, 'When you pray, say: "Father, hallowed be your name ..."' (Luke 11:2).

REFLECTION

'I open my mouth and pant, longing for your commands. Turn to me and have mercy on me, as you always do to those who love your name' (Ps. 119:131–132). The psalmist both longs for God's word and confesses his need for mercy, as the people do in Nehemiah 9. Why not pray along those lines?

DAY 21

READ Nehemiah 9:7–31

The main part of this great prayer is taken up with a review of Israel's history. It is packed with quotations and allusions to earlier parts of Scripture – clearly all their recent Bible study has had some effect!

As they look back, we see a pattern and a contrast that is not hard to spot! What is God like?

- He is completely faithful. He keeps the promises he makes to Abraham and his family (vv. 7–8). He has kept them through the Exodus and the wanderings in the wilderness (vv. 9–15), and through the conquest of Canaan (vv. 22–25).
- He is wonderfully generous. He supplied for his people (v. 15 – quoted by Jesus in John 6:31), he gave them his good word to live by (vv. 13–14), and he provided them with a ready-made paradise (v. 25).
- He is astonishingly merciful. He has disciplined them for their sins (v. 30b), but he has not destroyed them completely (v. 31), even though he could very justly have done so many times over! His nature is always to have mercy (vv. 17, 19, 27, 31).

And what have they been like? Proud, disobedient, thankless and hard-hearted (vv. 16, 26, 29)! The book of Hebrews tells us that Israel had one big root problem: unbelief (Heb. 3:12–19). They simply have not believed what God has said to them. There is a warning for us!

REFLECTION

All of this they freely confess! If we were to look back – over our lives (even over the last week!), or perhaps over church history – how would we see the same patterns and contrasts? What lingering unbelief might we need to confess to God?

DAY 22

READ Nehemiah 9:32–37

The people sum up the situation, confessing, 'In all that has happened to us, you have remained righteous; you have acted faithfully, while we acted wickedly' (v. 33). Like Nehemiah did, they include themselves in the failure to obey God's commandments. The people acknowledge that because of their wickedness (vv. 34–35), they are now slaves in their own land (vv. 36–37). God has handed them over to such punishment, as he always said he would.

But now they ask for mercy: 'Now therefore ... do not let all this hardship seem trifling in your eyes – the hardship that has come on us' (v. 32). That is a plea for God's favour. That is always the right thing to do when we realise our sin!

Yet what hope could there be for such a wicked people? How do they dare ask for God's mercy after all their wickedness?! The answer is not because they deserve it. The answer is in God's character: 'our God, the great God, mighty and awesome, who keeps his covenant of love ...' (v. 32). They have been reading God's word. They know that God has promised to re-establish them in the promised land if they turn back to him. They know that God has promised to show mercy to those who cry out to him for it.

In terms of righteousness before a holy God, we are no better off than they: 'all have sinned and fall short of the glory of God' (Rom. 3:23). How will we ever find mercy? What hope is there for a world handed over to judgement? Mercy may still be found in the great, mighty and awesome God who shows steadfast covenantal love to all who call on him. We do not deserve God's mercy but we may indeed ask God for it, because he has promised to show it through and in Jesus Christ.

REFLECTION

Restoration to the land of Canaan was only the 'shadow' promise. The real promise is eternal life in the new creation! And this is what God promises to give to everyone who asks for his mercy in Jesus (John 6:40). Praise to our God – there is none like him!

DAY 23

READ Nehemiah 9:38 – 10:29

There is a deliberate order to what happens in these chapters. The people have heard God's word, confessed their sins, and grasped hold of his mercy – and only now, 'in view of all this', do they make a 'binding agreement, putting it in writing' to live for God (9:38). This is the gospel pattern: 'I urge you, brothers and sisters, in view of God's mercy, to offer your bodies as a living sacrifice, holy and pleasing to God – this is your true and proper worship' (Rom. 12:1).

The leaders of the people seal the document (10:1–27) – Nehemiah as ever showing the way by going first. How right and appropriate it is that the leaders of God's people do this!

The rest of the people follow suit in entering into the covenant (10:28–29). They bind themselves to 'a curse and an oath to follow the Law of God given through Moses the servant of God and to obey carefully all the commands, regulations and decrees of the LORD our Lord' (v. 29).

Their intention is to obey God's word to the letter. 'Obedience' is not a popular word in our culture. But the Bible has no problem with obedience! It is the mark of a true believer – because if we believe that what God says is true, we will do it! Paul calls it 'the obedience of faith' (Rom. 1:5, ESV).

The people, after receiving God's mercy by faith, commit to doing his commandments by faith. That is their intention – and it should be ours, too. Will they fail, and have to ask for God's forgiveness? Yes! Will we? Of course! Nevertheless, Jesus himself says, 'If you love me, you will keep my commandments' (John 14:15, ESV).

REFLECTION

Read 1 John 2:1–6. How serious are you about obeying his word, in light of his mercy?

DAY 24

READ Nehemiah 10:30–39

In addition to their general commitment to obedience, there are three specific obligations to the covenant the people make:

1. They will not marry outside of the people of God (v. 30).
2. They will not abuse the weekly and seven-yearly Sabbath rests (v. 31).
3. They will not neglect the recently rebuilt temple and all its accompaniments (vv. 32–39).

Why these three things in particular? We aren't told! Perhaps they encapsulate all of their key relationships: to one another, the land and to God. Or perhaps they are especially conscious of particularly disastrous past failure in these areas.[8] But remember these three things when we come to the end of the book.

It is always good to refresh our serious obedience to God's word in general, and at times to renew commitment to specific things that God has commanded. Their commitments here will not look the same for us, although the New Testament picks up many of the same principles. For example:

- God forbade them from intermarrying with the nations largely because it would (and did!) lead them into idolatry. God's people are still to marry within God's people, and to avoid partnership with what leads to idolatry (2 Cor. 6:14–18).
- A key function of the Sabbath was that it provided an opportunity for God's people to rest from ordinary work and meet together around God's word. The New Testament makes absolutely clear that we are not to neglect such times (Heb. 10:24–25).
- Whilst we no longer give to the upkeep of the temple in Jerusalem, we are to give to the work of the gospel, which proclaims Christ, the true temple – that is, the true place where God and human beings may meet (2 Cor. 9:6–15).

REFLECTION

Ultimately, the themes of marriage, Sabbath rest, and temple all come together in Christ and his relationship to his church (see, for example, Rev. 19:7–8; Matt. 11:28–29; John 2:18–22). Here is a call to devotion to Christ and his people!

DAY 25

READ Nehemiah 11:1–36

In the next two chapters, we find the people starting to live out all that they have just heard and said. There is a hugely positive feel to this part of the book! Nehemiah 11 returns to the subject of the population of Jerusalem. The city appears to be well supplied with leaders (v. 1), but most of the rest of the people are spread sparsely around the other towns.

So one in ten of the people are chosen by lot to move to 'Jerusalem, the holy city' (v. 1 – a striking phrase!). And look how the rest of the people encourage their fellow Jews: 'The people commended [or 'blessed', ESV] all who volunteered to live in Jerusalem' (v. 2). The people who cheerfully move to Jerusalem receive the commendation of their brothers for their self-sacrifice. We too need the encouragement of one another to keep doing what is pleasing to God at cost to self! We are to commend one another when we do what is right.

The encouragements continue in verses 3–36. Particular focus is given to the priests, and to the tribes of Judah and Benjamin. Notice especially the reference to the sons of Perez in verse 6; he was the son of Judah, born through awful sin (see Gen. 38), but through God's grace was an ancestor of King David. There is no Davidic king on the throne in Nehemiah's day, but amazingly the family line is still alive: there is hope that a king will arise! And he does. Perez is also an ancestor of Jesus Christ (see Matt. 1:3; Luke 3:33).

A number of the towns of the old kingdom of Judah are then mentioned (vv. 25–36). All of this calls to mind the great days of David and Solomon.[9] But we can also see how small and feeble it all is compared to those days. There is still a long way to go.

REFLECTION

We too have a way to go yet. God's people are not supposed go the way of the cross alone: 'Therefore encourage one another and build each other up, just as in fact you are doing' (1 Thes. 5:11).Who are the people you know who need your encouragement?

DAY 26

READ Nehemiah 12:1–26

This section focuses on the priests and Levites. To begin with there are listed (by their family names) those who were the first to come up out of exile (vv. 1–11). Next are others from a generation after that (vv. 12–21) and then the one after that (vv. 22–25), and so down to Nehemiah's own day (v. 26).

As we have seen, the priestly tribe of Levi had various duties, such as teaching the Scriptures and offering the sacrifices. Here the unnamed writer of these verses recalls that King David, 'the man of God', commanded that the Levites also took the lead 'to praise and to give thanks… watch by watch …' (v. 24, ESV). Again, there is a strong element of continuity with the pre-exile days (see 1 Chr. 23–25 for the details). The priestly tribe was to take it in shifts to ensure ceaseless praise was lifted to God in the temple.

Some of these responsibilities have particular application for the leaders of God's people today – of course, it is right that the elders of the church take the lead in teaching the Scriptures, and in offering to God the praise that is due to his name. But the New Testament tells us that it is Jesus who is the real 'worship leader'! It is he who brings us into the presence of God. It is he who leads the people of God in praise to God for the salvation that he himself has achieved (Heb. 2:10–12). And so, in and through Jesus, it is the joy and privilege of every believer to lift continual praise to God: 'Through him then let us continually offer up a sacrifice of praise to God, that is, the fruit of lips that acknowledge his name' (Heb. 13:15, ESV).

REFLECTION

What a wonderful thing to be brought into the presence of the holy God by Jesus! May our lips be quick to praise our God and to acknowledge his name.

DAY 27

READ Nehemiah 12:27–43

The ministries of Ezra and Nehemiah overlapped significantly. It is hard to imagine two more determined, godly men leading the church! Between them, they are the driving force behind this revival. We should pray that God would raise up such leaders in our own generations.

In these verses (narrated once more by Nehemiah), the newly built wall is dedicated. Many are gathered together for what promises to be a joyful occasion (vv. 27–29), and appropriate 'purification' preparations are made (v. 30).

The leaders and singers take their place: 'I had the leaders of Judah go up on top of the wall. I also assigned two large choirs to give thanks' (v. 31). No doubt the rest of the people watch on excitedly! The two groups start off in opposite directions around the wall, Ezra going with one group, Nehemiah with the other. The choirs sing praise – perhaps they had Psalm 48:12–14 in mind. They meet once again on the other side, at the temple (v. 40).

It must have been quite a spectacle! All the people rejoice. Nehemiah notes, 'The sound of rejoicing in Jerusalem could be heard far away' (v. 43). We have reached the high point of the book – it seems like all of God's promises of restoration have been fulfilled!

We saw much rejoicing in chapter 8 too. How right it is when God's people rejoice in his mighty works of grace! That is how it will be at the coming of Jesus; that will be the occasion of supreme, eternal praise. Read, for example, the songs of Revelation 19.

But such joy should be a mark of God's people now too, as we wait. Trace the theme of 'rejoicing' in a letter like Philippians. Paul is always utterly clear that his rejoicing is 'in the Lord' – in Christ and all that Christ has done. We so quickly rejoice in other things. May our joy be rooted in the Lord.

REFLECTION

Are our church gatherings marked by this kind of joy in the Lord, as we 'walk over' the gospel together? Is our joy be obvious to all – 'heard far away', as it were – as it was in Nehemiah 12:43?

DAY 28

READ Nehemiah 12:44 – 13:3

These verses are a little tricky to pinpoint chronologically.[10] They are not from Nehemiah's pen, but are again by an unnamed narrator. They seem to work as a summary of all the reform that has happened since chapter 8.

This writer is particularly keen to stress the continuity of these reforms with the Israel of before the exile; we have seen that before. This is very much an attempt to return to the days of David and Solomon (12:45–46). The fact that some achievements have been made towards that would have been a real encouragement to the original readers!

We make much of certain times in church history such as the Reformation (especially as we celebrate its 500th anniversary). We rejoice in 'reformed theology' and fight hard to preserve it. We are encouraged and humbled by those men and women of the faith, and we long to have something of their zeal and sacrificial spirit. We remember with gratitude what the Lord did through their faith in the face of great adversity (just like he did with the Israelites, 13:2).

And so we should! But of course the ultimate authority behind everything was the word of God. We shouldn't simply want to go back in time because we think things were purer and better then – they weren't! Rather our desire should be that we are shaped by the Scriptures, as they were.

It is the same here in Nehemiah's day. Their idea isn't to do all these things simply because that's what they did in the glorious old days! Rather it is because they too long to be shaped by God's word (12:44; 13:1, 3, echoing Deut. 23:3–5).

The 'reformation' of the people of God in Nehemiah's day began with God's word (in chapter 8) and continued under it. But it is worth us noting that this is a clear return to the *old covenant*. And so – with our New Testament eyes – we can see that this cannot truly be the end of the story.

REFLECTION

The word of God must continue to be the ultimate authority for his people! Whatever (good) role our church traditions and histories may play, we must test it all by the Scriptures: 'Sanctify them by the truth; your word is truth' (John 17:17).

DAY 29

READ Nehemiah 13:4–31

And indeed it is not the end of the story. Nehemiah 13 is amongst the most bitter chapters in the Bible. Nehemiah tells us in verse 6 that, after a twelve-year stint as governor in Judah, he returns to King Artaxerxes. Then, after a time, he comes back once more to Jerusalem – for an unspecified time, perhaps the rest of his life. But he comes back to discover that:

- They are neglecting the temple and everything that goes with it (vv. 4–14). Tobiah (who is still at large and dangerous, as is Sanballat – v. 28) is even using a room in the temple courts as a private sitting room (v. 7).
- They are breaking the Sabbath (vv. 15–22). They are trading on the Sabbath day, even in Jerusalem itself and even with foreign nations (v. 16).
- They are intermarrying with foreign nations (vv. 23–27). This is so much the case that some of their children are starting to lose their identity as the people of God (vv. 23–24).

These are the three very things the people bound themselves to in chapter 10 – even calling a curse on themselves should they fail! How did it all go so wrong so quickly?

Nehemiah sorts it all out in his characteristic manner. He heatedly confronts the people with their sin (vv. 11, 17–18, 25). Then, foreshadowing Christ (see John 2:13–17), he takes stern action (vv. 8–9, 11–13, 19–22, 25–28 – you can feel his frustration!), with plenty of reminders of past sins and their consequences. And, as ever, he prays about it all (vv. 14, 22, 29, 31).

Nehemiah deals with the problem ... in a way. But it's clear that the real problem, the problem of the sinful heart, has not been sorted. Nehemiah, great man of God though he truly is, ultimately can't bring about a lasting solution. The book ends on this sour note. The question has to be: 'What now?'

REFLECTION

What a devastating place to end the Old Testament story. The great restoration has not really happened after all! As so often, the Old Testament leaves us crying for someone who can permanently sort out the mess ...

DAY 30

READ Hebrews 12:1–29

Four hundred years later, things are no better. In fact, they are worse! The people are still in a sinful mess. The great Davidic King promised in 2 Samuel 7 seems to be nowhere. The city is ruled and occupied by the Romans (who would soon destroy it completely).

Simply restoring the old covenant will not do, especially since God had promised a completely new one (Jer. 31:31–34). Simply rebuilding the old Jerusalem also will not do. What is really needed – and what God promised – is a completely new Jerusalem, 'whose architect and builder is God' himself (Heb. 11:10)!

Nehemiah could not truly rebuild either the place of God or the people of God. But in Nehemiah we are dealing in shadows. Hebrews 12 tells us of the reality. In verses 18–24, the writer contrasts the physical nature of the old covenant to the (currently) spiritual nature of the new.

Amazingly, the writer says that we *have already* come to the new Jerusalem by faith in Jesus! The Lord Jesus is building a great city of God's people, which will one day appear in physical form ... But, spiritually speaking, we're already there!

The Jews in Nehemiah's day were redeemed from exile. They had experienced a partial fulfilment of what God had promised. Yet they were still very obviously waiting for the full reality.

We are not so different. We are redeemed from the 'exile' of sin. We have a partial fulfilment of all that God has promised us. But we are still waiting for the fullness – the day when the physical reality matches the spiritual.

REFLECTION

What should we do whilst we wait? Nehemiah himself would heartily affirm the answer of Hebrews 12! We look to our founder and leader: Jesus, who has endured the cross and is now exalted (v 2). We battle sin (vv. 1, 3–4). We submit ourselves to God (vv. 5–11). We persevere (vv. 12–17). We listen to God's words (vv. 25–27). And we worship God with reverent thankfulness (vv. 28–29).

DAY 31

READ Revelation 21:1 – 22:5

In truth, 'the joy of the whole earth ... the city of the Great King' (Ps. 48:2) is not a description of Nehemiah's Jerusalem. But the new Jerusalem that John sees coming down from God (Rev. 21:2) is truly that! There God himself will dwell in person with all his redeemed people in perfection forever (21:3–4). Nehemiah will be there! All God's enemies will be judged (21:8), so that nothing evil will ever threaten this city (21:27). There will be no Tobiahs or Sanballats there!

This 'Holy City' (21:2; remember Neh. 11:1!) is then described (21:9 – 22:5). It has a magnificent wall (21:12, 18–21). And it has gates that never need be shut (21:25) – what a contrast to Nehemiah 7:3. There is no temple because the Lamb himself is there (21:22) – there is no need for a temple if you have the Lord Jesus! It is lit with the glory of God (21:23). Kings and nations will glory in it (21:24, 26). God's people have a perfect relationship with God and each other there (22:3–4) – there is no more sin. And they will reign with him (22:5). There will never be another Fall. It is completely perfect!

This holy city is where salvation history is really heading. That is our future as believers: the people of God, in the place of God, in the presence of God, forever and ever.

REFLECTION

Two prayers would seem an appropriate way for us to end. The first is Nehemiah's own prayer in 13:14, 22, 31: 'Remember me'. He asks God to remember how he has served him. But he does not think he has earned God's favour. He knows he needs mercy. And he knows that God has promised it and will not forget. So he prays, 'Remember me with favour, my God' (13:31). Or, as the thief on the cross put it, 'Jesus, remember me when you come into your kingdom' (Luke 23:42). Jesus will not forget to show his mercy to those who ask according to his promise.

The second is that of John in Revelation 22:20: 'Amen. Come, Lord Jesus'! That is the true longing of all believers. Reading Nehemiah should increase that longing.

HISTORICAL BACKGROUND TO NEHEMIAH

Historically, Ezra–Nehemiah is one book. It's really a compilation of different sources – an account of the initial return from exile in Babylon and the rebuilding of the temple (Ezra 1–6); various letters (for example in Ezra 4); various lists from the archives (for example in Nehemiah 3); material by other unnamed narrators; and the memoirs of those two great men of God, Ezra and Nehemiah.

The two books span quite a time frame: the initial return from exile happened in the 530s BC, but Nehemiah and Ezra were active a century or so later in the 450s–420s BC. At some point shortly after this, an editor – very possibly Ezra himself, as Jewish tradition has it – put all the material together into this one compilation. (The book of Psalms was edited and compiled around the same time.)

A more detailed timeline of Judah is as follows:

- 930 BC: the united kingdom of Israel splits into two – 'Israel' and 'Judah'.
- 597/596 BC: many Jews are deported to Babylon by King Nebuchadnezzar; Jeremiah, Daniel and Ezekiel are active just before/during the exile.
- 587/586 BC: a second deportation of people to Babylon occurs; King Nebuchadnezzar reduces Jerusalem to ruins.
- 539 BC: the Persian emperor Cyrus conquers Babylon and allows the Jews to return home. The first return from exile happens under the Jewish leaders Zerubbabel and Joshua.
- 538 BC onwards: the temple is rebuilt; Haggai and Zechariah are active at this time.
- 458 BC onwards: Ezra comes to Jerusalem with a further group of returning exiles. An attempt to rebuild the wall is stopped by Artaxerxes.
- 445 BC onwards: Nehemiah comes to Jerusalem and rebuilds the walls. He stays as governor for twelve years; Nehemiah and Ezra together lead the people in covenant renewal.
- 433 BC: Nehemiah returns to the Persian emperor.
- 433 BC onwards: at some point Nehemiah comes back again to Jerusalem and remains for an unspecified time; Malachi is probably active during or shortly after this second visit.

Together with the writing of the prophets Haggai, Zechariah and Malachi, Ezra–Nehemiah as a whole gives us our picture of the Jews after their return from exile: the rebuilding and renewal of Jerusalem, and the successes, struggles and sins of God's people.

We may wonder why the walls of Jerusalem are such an important issue for Nehemiah. In part the answer is obvious – the wall of a city was its security. The Bible even uses city walls as a metaphor for spiritual strength (for example, 'Like a city whose walls are broken through is a person who lacks self-control,' Prov. 25:28).

But the walls of Jerusalem have further significance because of their location. Salvation history can be thought of as the people of God, in the place of God, in the presence of God.[11] That was the situation in the Garden of Eden. When this was lost at the Fall, God graciously promised to restore it one day. Salvation is not complete without those three inseparable aspects.

Ever since King David's day, Jerusalem ('Zion') was very much seen as the place of God where his people could live in his presence. Many psalms celebrate Zion as the place of joy for God's people but of terror for his enemies (see Ps.46:4–7). But if the place of God is in ruins, then the people of God are in disgrace. (It was part of God's judgement on their sins which had led to the exile – Lam. 2:8–9). That is why Nehemiah was so upset that the walls were still a pile of rubble. And he was desperate for this to be sorted out because the prophets had announced that, after the punishment of the exile, everything would be gloriously restored.

Passages like Ezekiel 36 and Jeremiah 31–33 provide a striking backdrop for what happens in Ezra–Nehemiah because all three elements are dealt with: the presence of God (the temple and sacrificial system) in Ezra 1–6; the place of God (Jerusalem and its walls) in Nehemiah 1–6; and the people of God (the repopulation of Jerusalem with people under God's word) in Ezra 7–10 and Nehemiah 7–13. People, place and presence are re-established after the return from exile – to some degree! But we're still left waiting for the real thing ...

REFERENCES

[1] Derek Kidner, *Ezra & Nehemiah*, part of the Tyndale Old Testament Commentaries series (IVP, 1979; reprinted 2009), p. 83. Kidner's short commentary is extremely helpful and insightful.

[2] See, for example, Genesis 8:1. God could hardly have 'forgotten' Noah!

[3] Derek Kidner, *Ezra & Nehemiah*, p. 86. This is just one of the many clear shadows of Jesus that we find in Nehemiah (see Rom. 8:34)!

[4] The Persian Empire in Artaxerxes' day ruled unchallenged from Macedonia in the north to India in the east to Egypt in the south, and crucially to Israel in the west. It is estimated that an astonishing 44% of the world population then lived under Persian rule – the largest percentage of any empire in history!

[5] Sanballat with the Samaritans is to the north, Tobiah with the Ammonies to the east, Geshem with the Arabs to the south, and now the Ashdodites to the west.

[6] In fact, Ezra had come to Jerusalem for the very purpose of teaching the people (Ezra 7). Many Jews by this time would have spoken Aramaic rather than Hebrew, so part of this explanation might well have been simply translating the Scriptures into a language people could understand!

[7] For more background on the Feast of Booths, see Numbers 29:12–40; Deuteronomy 16:13–15 and 31:9–13; and Zechariah 14:16–19. Jesus himself goes up to this feast in John 7:1.

[8] See, for example, 1 Kings 11:1–13 on marriage; Jeremiah 17:19–27 on the Sabbath; and 2 Chronicles 29:3–11 on the temple. These themes resurface in Ezra–Nehemiah several times, so they are clearly on the minds of the returned exiles.

[9] Some of the towns listed in verses 25–36 were well outside the influence of Nehemiah's small province. They are perhaps included for this sense of continuity – and in hopeful expectation.

[10] See Kidner, *Ezra & Nehemiah*, pp. 140–41.

[11] Or it could be summarised even as: the perfect people of God, in the perfect place of God, in the perfect presence of God!